STECK-VAUGHN

Comprehension Skills

CONCLUSION

LEVEL
E

Linda Ward Beech
Tara McCarthy
Donna Townsend

STECK-VAUGHN
COMPANY
A Subsidiary of National Education Corporation

Executive Editor:	Diane Sharpe
Project Editor:	Melinda Veatch
Design Coordinator:	Sharon Golden
Project Design:	Howard Adkins Communications
Cover Illustration:	Rhonda Childress
Photographs:	©COMSTOCK INC. / Tom Grill

ISBN 0-8114-7852-1

6 7 8 9 0 VP 02 01 00 99 98 97

To draw a conclusion, you have to be a detective. You must put all the clues together in order to find the answer.

Look at the picture. The woman in the picture is working. What is her job? Suppose you knew that people with her job cannot be afraid of heights. Would that change your conclusion? Which parts of the picture give you clues about what she is doing?

What Is a Conclusion?

A conclusion is a decision you make after thinking about all the information you have. In a story the writer may not state all of his or her ideas. When you read you often have to hunt for clues so that you can understand the whole story. By putting all of the writer's clues together, you can draw a conclusion about the information.

There are many stories in this book. You will draw conclusions based on the stories you read.

Try It!

Read this story about jellyfish. Think about the information it gives you.

---◆---

Don't touch that colorful balloon floating in the sea. It's probably a jellyfish. Hundreds of tentacles, or long arms, hang below the "balloon." The arms can sting fish and people and sometimes even kill them. At times you can see small fish swimming under the jellyfish. Even though the fish may bump into the poisonous arms of the jellyfish, they remain unharmed.

What conclusion can you draw? Write a conclusion on the lines below.

_____

_____

You might have written something, such as "The jellyfish hurts people but does not hurt small fish" or "Small fish are not bothered by the poison of the jellyfish." You can draw these conclusions from the story. The fourth sentence tells that the jellyfish can hurt or kill people. The last sentence says that the jellyfish is poisonous. It also tells that small fish can bump into the jellyfish without getting hurt. From these clues you can draw the above conclusions.

Using What You Know

Read the stories on this page. Hunt for clues that will help you draw a conclusion about each school subject being described.

This is my favorite subject. I am learning to read maps. I can tell you what the largest bodies of water are called. I can name the seven continents. I can even tell you what percent of the earth is covered by water.

I am studying _____.

This subject is hard but very useful. My teacher talks about numbers and uses many symbols. There are many kinds of problems to solve. It was easy learning the multiplication tables. Long division is another matter.

I am studying _____.

This subject is very important because it is the study of language. I study nouns, verbs, and all the parts of speech. I learn to put words together in order to make complete sentences. I am learning how to write well.

I am studying _____.

This is a fun subject for me because I love to draw. I am able to play with pencils, charcoal, and all kinds of paint. I like trying out different colors and designs.

I am studying _____.

To check your answers, turn to page 62.

Practice Drawing Conclusions

This book asks you to draw conclusions from the information, or clues, in the stories. Look at another example.

◆

Crocodiles sometimes eat other crocodiles — even their own young. They attack and eat large land animals, such as water buffalo, that come to the swamp to drink water. Crocodiles hold their victims underwater until they drown.

_C_ **1.** From this story you can tell that
- **A.** crocodiles attack only when they are scared
- **B.** crocodiles are very particular about what they eat
- **C.** crocodiles have very strong jaws
- **D.** people shouldn't be afraid of crocodiles

The correct answer is **C.** But the answer does not appear in the story. The last sentence says "Crocodiles hold their victims underwater until they drown." The second sentence begins, "They attack and eat large land animals." From this information you can conclude that crocodiles must have strong jaws in order to attack and hold their victims down long enough to drown them.

Sometimes a question asks about something you *cannot* tell from a story. Read the example that follows.

◆

The first matchbook was made in 1892. But matchbooks were unsafe until about 1914. Today many people collect matchbooks as a hobby. Collectors enjoy sorting their matchbooks according to the places they come from, such as hotels, restaurants, and airlines.

_____ **2.** From the story you <u>cannot</u> tell
- **A.** when matchbooks were invented
- **B.** what the first matchbook cover was like
- **C.** how collectors sort matchbooks
- **D.** when matchbooks became safe to use

To check your answer, turn to page 62.

How to Use This Book

Read the stories in this book. Answer the question to each story.

When you finish reading and answering the questions, check your answers by looking at pages 59 through 61. Tear out the answer pages and fold them to the unit you are checking. Write the number of correct answers in the score box at the top of the unit page. After you finish the stories, work through "Think and Apply" on pages 56 through 58.

Hints for Better Reading

◆ Read the question carefully. Each question is different. Does the question use the word *not* or the contraction *n't*?

◆ Sometimes the clue to the correct answer lies in the middle of the story. As you look for the answer, read the whole story again.

◆ Read all the answers before choosing the correct one. Sometimes there seems to be more than one correct answer. But only one of them really fits the clues in the story.

Challenge Yourself

Read each story and answer the questions. The answers you did not choose are conclusions that you *cannot* draw from the story. Write another conclusion you cannot draw.

1. One night during World War II, a duck in a city park in Freiburg, Germany, began squawking and flapping its wings. The duck had done this once before when bombs were dropped. This time, people heard the duck and ran for cover. Soon the bombing began. Today there is a statue of the duck in the park. It died in the attack.

2. Mack Sennett was an early film director who was famous for his silent comedies. Sennett's films were about the Keystone Cops. The Keystone Cops ignored the logic of everyday life. They seldom arrested anyone. If they did, it was the wrong person. The girls in Sennett's movies fell in love with ugly men instead of handsome ones. His films often ended with awful scenes, but at least no one got hurt.

3. Do you ever awaken right before the alarm clock rings? Experts know that people have "clocks" inside their bodies. The clock divides time into about 24 hours. Jet lag, or feeling tired and grumpy after traveling by plane, is a result of upsetting that inner clock.

4. Many movies show burglars studying a place before striking. Movies also show burglars picking locks with great skill. But police departments say that most burglars are very crude. They look for unlocked doors. If they don't find any, they just break down the door, force the lock, or break the window. Then they work fast.

5. The Baseball Hall of Fame is in Cooperstown, New York. This site was chosen because it is where Abner Doubleday said that he invented the game in 1839. But baseball began in England. It started from a game called rounders. The word *baseball* is mentioned in English books as early as 1798.

_____ **1.** This story has a sad twist because
- **A.** people didn't pay attention to the duck's warnings
- **B.** the bombing began just before the duck made noise
- **C.** the duck was killed in the attack
- **D.** the statue doesn't look anything like the duck

_____ **2.** The actors in Mack Sennett's films did not
- **A.** have to speak
- **B.** like working
- **C.** laugh much at work
- **D.** fall in love often

_____ **3.** From this story you can tell that jet lag
- **A.** happens when a person's inner clock is off schedule
- **B.** has nothing to do with the body's inner clock
- **C.** goes away after your watch is reset
- **D.** is something from which experts seldom suffer

_____ **4.** From this story you can tell that
- **A.** the police have no way to stop burglars
- **B.** burglars are usually skillful at their job
- **C.** burglars plan robberies carefully
- **D.** burglars in movies are not true-to-life

_____ **5.** This story suggests that Abner Doubleday
- **A.** began the game of _rounders_
- **B.** coined the word _baseball_ but not the game
- **C.** invented the game but not the word _baseball_
- **D.** received credit for something he didn't really do

1. Jim clutched the wheel so tightly that his knuckles stuck out against his skin. The woman next to him turned the key. She said, "Now just start out slowly down the street. To change direction you need to turn the wheel only slightly." Jim pressed his foot down carefully.

2. Roberta put the key into the slot and turned it. She pulled out four envelopes that were inside the little box. She flipped through the first three quickly, muttering "bill" at each one. When she reached the fourth envelope, she stopped. Then she grinned and ripped the flap open.

3. The first drop sent up a tiny cloud of dust and then disappeared. A rattlesnake slithered away from the unexpected sight. More drops followed, but they too were quickly lost in the dry sand. Then the drops increased. Puddles began to form among the cactus plants.

4. It was six o'clock by the time they reached Topeka, Kansas. Jed announced that they were now halfway there. "Just two more days," he said, "and we'll be swimming in the Pacific Ocean." He said it to cheer up the kids, but they were so tired of being in the car that nothing could have raised their spirits.

5. As they came outside, Marianne told Cathy that the ending had surprised her. Cathy said the ending hadn't surprised her, but she didn't understand why the police took so long to question the maid. Marianne asked Cathy if she was hungry, but Cathy said she had eaten too much popcorn.

_____ **1.** You can tell from this story that Jim
   A. is teaching the woman to drive
   B. is relaxed and confident
   C. is taking driving lessons from the woman
   D. is leaving the dock in a motorboat

_____ **2.** You can tell that Roberta probably received
   A. many letters from a friend named Bill
   B. three bills
   C. money in the fourth envelope
   D. quite a bit of mail every day

_____ **3.** The story is a description of
   A. rain falling in a desert after a dry period
   B. a sprinkler system in a zoo
   C. someone watering a lawn
   D. a storm beginning in the mountains

_____ **4.** You can tell that the family
   A. is moving to a new town
   B. has already been on the road a few days
   C. is moving from Topeka, Kansas
   D. has never seen the Pacific Ocean

_____ **5.** You can conclude that Marianne and Cathy
   A. have just finished a meal at a restaurant
   B. have just met
   C. are police officers discussing a case
   D. have just seen a movie together

1. John was once the King of England. Because he liked to hunt, he arranged to have a hunting camp built in the village of Gotham. The people of Gotham believed that the royal hunting camp would raise taxes. They also thought that there would be fewer animals for them to hunt. So when the king's builders came, the people played a trick on them. They all acted as if they were crazy. It worked! The king decided against building a hunting camp there.

2. Today skiing is a sport. But long ago, hunters used skis to chase animals. In Norway there is a rock carving made about four thousand years ago that shows two hunters on skis.

3. Natural rubber comes from trees that grow in warm climates. Native Americans shaped rubber into balls that they used in games. They also dripped liquid rubber over some of their clothes and shoes, which made the clothes and shoes handy on rainy days. The rubber made the clothing waterproof.

4. Long ago, people in Greece tried explaining through legend why the sun seemed to move across the sky. The Greeks said that a god flew across the sky in his golden chariot. At sunset the god took the chariot to the river that was believed to circle the earth. The god traveled east through the night. At sunrise he drove his carriage into the clouds once more.

5. Bowling is a very old game. The ancient Egyptians bowled more than seven thousand years ago. Later a few kings of England forbade people to bowl. They claimed that it was too harmless as a game. It did not prepare people for war as well as archery did.

_____ **1.** The people of Gotham acted crazy because

     A. they liked to play tricks on hunters

     B. they were afraid of kings

     C. they did not have to pay taxes

     D. they did not like the king's idea

_____ **2.** Skis were once most useful for people who

     A. liked to make rock carvings

     B. wanted to find food

     C. enjoyed having fun in the snow

     D. took vacations in Norway

_____ **3.** A shirt coated with rubber

     A. was made of tree bark

     B. was worn at ball games

     C. would keep a person dry

     D. could be made into shoes

_____ **4.** Ancient legends were stories that

     A. explained natural events

     B. children enjoyed hearing

     C. explained the uses of chariots

     D. told where rivers ran

_____ **5.** This story suggests that

     A. English kings felt games served serious purposes

     B. the Egyptians used bowling balls in war

     C. bowling was a popular game in France

     D. archery was more fun than bowling

1. Why do people sneeze? Scientists aren't sure why, but they know that sneezing can be a sign of illness. The Greeks at one time believed that one of their gods had invented sneezing. The early Romans believed that sneezing helped people make smart decisions. People in Europe thought that sneezing was a symbol of good health. So any patient who sneezed three times was always released from the hospital.

2. People in England used to hold many handwriting contests. The winner usually received a gold pen. In one contest the judges could not decide between two men who wrote beautifully. The judges looked at the handwriting samples for days. They found that one of the men had forgotten to dot an *i*. Because of this the other man walked away with the gold pen.

3. When our country was new, most people lived on farms. About 95 out of every 100 people made their living by growing food. They ate the food they grew and sold whatever was left over to the people in cities. Today only about 2 out of every 100 people are farmers.

4. People who visit Washington, D.C., often want souvenirs. They want a flag that has flown over the dome of the Capitol. To fill these requests, a flag crew takes about three hundred flags to the dome every day. They run each flag up the flagpole for a few seconds, and then they take the flag down. The flags are folded, stored, and given to visitors.

5. A famous poet sat down in a restaurant. A man working in the restaurant recognized the poet. "I will put my poems by the poet's plate," thought the worker. Later the poet read the worker's poems. The next day the worker's name was in the newspapers. His name was Langston Hughes.

1. From this story you can tell that

    A. sneezing has improved through the years
    B. the early Greeks were the first to sneeze
    C. ideas about sneezing have changed over time
    D. most people sneeze only three times

2. One man lost the contest because he

    A. did not want the gold pen
    B. could not write beautifully
    C. forgot an important part of a letter
    D. did not follow the rules of the contest

3. Over time, Americans have been

    A. eating less and less
    B. moving away from farms
    C. moving out of towns and cities
    D. buying more farmland

4. You can tell from the story that

    A. many flags fly over the Capitol every day
    B. most people cannot tell one flag from another
    C. the flag crew does not like its work
    D. everyone has respect for the American flag

5. You can conclude that the famous poet

    A. liked the restaurant
    B. did not like the worker's poems
    C. ate pizza
    D. liked the worker's poems

1. Pickles are made from cucumbers. People have been eating pickles for more than four thousand years. People in the United States eat more than one billion pounds of pickles each year. There is even a time for celebrating pickles. The third week in May is known as Pickle Week.

2. Jesse Owens was one of the greatest athletes of this century. He took part in the 1936 Olympics, in which he won four gold medals. But he won an even greater honor there. That year the Olympics were held in Berlin. The German leader was Adolph Hitler, who believed that white Germans were better than everyone else in the world. Because Owens was an African American, he wanted to prove Hitler wrong. With his great talent, Owens did just that.

3. On November 2 the Day of the Dead is observed in Mexico. According to Mexican legends, the dead return to life on this day. To greet the dead, families hold picnics at their graves. First, food is offered to the dead. Then the families finish the picnic in the graveyard.

4. A *gulf* is a body of water that is partly enclosed by land. The Gulf of Mexico is the biggest gulf in the world. It is just south of the United States. This gulf covers seven hundred thousand square miles of the earth's surface. It is one thousand miles wide from east to west. From north to south, the gulf is eight hundred miles wide.

5. Leslie Silko is a modern writer. She was born in New Mexico. She is part Pueblo, part white, and part Mexican. As a child she heard many Native American stories. She liked the legends of her people. She also learned the customs of her tribe. Today she uses that knowledge to write stories. She wants everyone to know about the history of Native Americans.

_____ **1.** You can tell from the story that
- A. Pickle Week is in March
- B. people in the United States like pickles
- C. pickles are a recent invention
- D. cucumbers are made from pickles

_____ **2.** From the story you can tell that
- A. Jesse Owens agreed with Adolph Hitler
- B. Adolph Hitler liked Jesse Owens
- C. Jesse Owens had a special reason for winning
- D. Adolph Hitler was an African American

_____ **3.** The story suggests that
- A. picnics in graveyards are more fun than those in parks
- B. dead people really do return to life
- C. the Day of the Dead is held in springtime
- D. people in Mexico like to remember the dead

_____ **4.** You can conclude that
- A. the Gulf of Mexico contains huge amounts of water
- B. a gulf is completely surrounded by land
- C. the Gulf of Mexico is a river
- D. the United States is south of the Gulf of Mexico

_____ **5.** The story suggests that Leslie Silko
- A. was born in New Jersey
- B. writes about fancy cloth
- C. forgot all her childhood stories
- D. takes pride in her Native American background

1. Alice Walker is a famous writer today. She was born in Georgia in 1944. As a child she was blind in one eye. This greatly affected her young life. Because she was African American, she was troubled by race problems, too. After college she joined the civil rights movement. She began writing and teaching. Today her stories deal mostly with the problems of women and racism.

2. The longest river in the world is the Nile. It runs through North Africa. The Nile is more than four thousand miles long. But the Nile is just one hundred miles longer than the Amazon River. The Amazon is found in South America.

3. Modern weddings are full of traditions. Some of these traditions date back to ancient times. Even today many brides wear veils when they marry. This comes from an ancient Spartan practice. At that time the bride used the veil to hide from evil spirits. Even the bridesmaids were meant to hide the bride away from evil spirits. The bride would surround herself with girls her own age in order to confuse the evil spirits. Only the groom could recognize her then.

4. The United States is made up of fifty states. Most of the state names are not English words. Many of the names of the states come from Native American words. For example, *Arkansas* is a Quapaw word that means "downstream people." *Texas* comes from a Caddo word meaning "friends." *Wisconsin* means "place of the beaver."

5. Have you ever heard cooks say that they have enough food to feed Coxey's army? This old saying has its roots in history. Jacob Coxey worked to help the homeless and the jobless. In 1894 he formed an "army" of jobless men. They marched to Washington, D.C. They wanted Congress to help the poor. But they never received any help. Instead, many of them were jailed for walking on the Capitol lawn.

_____ **1.** The story suggests that Alice Walker
   A. writes about her own problems in her stories
   B. was born in Oregon
   C. joined the civil rights movement in 1940
   D. became deaf as a child

_____ **2.** From the story you can tell that
   A. the Amazon is longer than the Nile
   B. the Nile is in South America
   C. the Nile and Amazon are very long rivers
   D. the Amazon is only one hundred miles long

_____ **3.** You can conclude that
   A. the groom is an evil spirit
   B. the Spartans were afraid of evil spirits
   C. evil spirits like wedding cakes
   D. bridesmaids help evil spirits find the bride

_____ **4.** You can tell from the story that
   A. Wisconsin probably had many beavers at one time
   B. *Texas* is an English word
   C. Arkansas is not a state in the United States
   D. the United States has 55 states

_____ **5.** The story suggests that
   A. Jacob Coxey did not like jobless people
   B. Coxey's army received help from Congress
   C. the marchers tried to eat the Capitol lawn
   D. Coxey's army didn't achieve its goal

1. The United States is a very large country. Only three countries are bigger in size. The Soviet Union is the biggest country in the world and covers more than eight million square miles. It is more than twice the size of the United States. Second in size is Canada. The third-largest country is China.

2. In 1978 Lorenzo Amato made a huge pizza. In fact, it was the biggest pizza ever made. It weighed more than eighteen thousand pounds and was topped with more than one thousand pounds of cheese. After it was baked, it was cut into sixty thousand pieces!

3. Adolfo Esquivel is a great believer in human rights. He lives in Argentina, where he is head of the Peace and Justice Service. This group works hard for the rights of all people. Sometimes the work proves dangerous. For his efforts Esquivel has been jailed and even tortured several times. But he continues his struggle. His work has paid off. He won the Nobel Peace Prize in 1980.

4. In Czechoslovakia, children celebrate the end of winter. But they do so in an unusual way. First they make a straw figure. The figure is a symbol of death called Smrt. The straw is decorated with colored rags and bits of eggshell. Then the children burn the straw figure. Sometimes they throw it into a river. After destroying Smrt the children wear flowers to welcome springtime.

5. William Taft was once president. He was different in many ways. He was the heaviest president ever. He weighed more than three hundred pounds. Taft was the first president to play golf. He was the first one to throw a ball to mark the start of baseball season. Taft died in 1930. He was laid to rest in Arlington National Cemetery. He was the first president to be buried there.

_____ **1.** You can conclude that

      A. Canada is smaller than the United States

      B. the Soviet Union is bigger than the earth

      C. China is bigger than Canada

      D. there are countries smaller than the United States

_____ **2.** The story suggests that

      A. Lorenzo's pizza fed many people

      B. the pizza was not very heavy

      C. Lorenzo's pizza tasted awful

      D. Lorenzo Amato hated making pizzas

_____ **3.** You can tell from the story that

      A. fighting for human rights is always fun

      B. Esquivel is willing to suffer for his beliefs

      C. Argentina is a state in the United States

      D. Esquivel gave up his struggle after being jailed

_____ **4.** The story suggests that

      A. the straw figure is a symbol of summer

      B. straw doesn't burn

      C. the flowers are a sign of springtime

      D. the Czech children hate to see winter end

_____ **5.** From the story you can tell that

      A. Taft began many presidential customs

      B. tennis was Taft's favorite game

      C. Taft was a small man

      D. President Taft is still alive

1. The Japanese celebrate an unusual custom on May 5. The event is called the Boys' Festival. On this day families fly giant, red-and-black kites in the shape of carp fish. These carp-shaped kites are intended to honor young sons. The event is meant to develop manly qualities in the boys. The carp was chosen as a symbol of strength. Each year the carp fights its way upstream to produce its young.

2. Today Emily Dickinson is known as one of America's greatest poets. She led a very private life. She spent much of her time alone and seldom visited others. All her writing was done in secret. In fact, her great talent in poetry was not discovered until after her death. Today her short poems are thought to be among the best in the English language.

3. The highest lake that can be traveled by big boats is in the Andes Mountains. It is called Lake Titicaca. The lake is more than two miles above sea level. The lake is also the largest one in South America. It is ten miles long and up to nine hundred feet deep.

4. Christopher Wren was a famous English architect. In 1666 a great fire swept through London. Much of the city was destroyed. Wren drew plans to rebuild London. But his plans were never used. However, he did play a key part in the repair of the city. He designed more than fifty new churches. He also helped with the construction of nearly every major building in the city.

5. Many couples celebrate wedding anniversaries. Certain years require special gifts. For example, a couple married for 1 year should be given a gift of paper. A couple married for 5 years ought to receive a gift of wood. For 25 years of marriage, a gift of silver is best. The usual gift for 50 years of marriage is something gold.

_____ **1.** You can conclude that

    A. carp kites can fly underwater

    B. strength is a worthy quality

    C. the carp is a weak fish

    D. the carp lays its eggs in the air

_____ **2.** The story suggests that Emily Dickinson

    A. liked having big parties

    B. was famous during her lifetime

    C. wrote stories about chickens

    D. never knew her fame as a poet

_____ **3.** From the story you can tell that

    A. Lake Titicaca is probably hard to get to

    B. Lake Titicaca is very small

    C. Lake Titicaca is full of sharks

    D. the Andes Mountains are located in Montana

_____ **4.** You can tell from the story that Christopher Wren

    A. knew little about construction

    B. drew plans to burn London

    C. worked hard to rebuild London

    D. was French

_____ **5.** The story suggests that

    A. the longer the marriage, the better the gift

    B. gold should be given after 5 years of marriage

    C. wood is always a good gift

    D. paper should be given after 1 week of marriage

1. Peter Salem was a soldier in the American Revolution. Salem was a slave, as were most African Americans at the time. But he was set free to join the army. He fought bravely at Concord and Lexington and was a hero at Bunker Hill. Salem took part in many more battles, too. After the war ended, the United States became a free nation. Salem became a free man.

2. Texas became a state in 1845. Before that time it was a nation that had its own laws and money. It was known as the Republic of Texas and is the only nation to have ever become a state.

3. Most babies learn to talk by imitating the sounds they hear. Babies first babble, and later they are able to say words. A new study on babies has made some amazing discoveries. The study shows that deaf babies with deaf parents also babble, but they babble with their hands. They imitate the sign language that their parents use.

4. In Greek legends Achilles was a mighty warrior. The Greeks were at war with the city of Troy. Achilles decided to join the battle. But his mother dreamed that he would die in the fight. To protect him she dipped him in the River Styx. But the water did not touch his heel where she held him. Achilles later went to fight in Troy. But there he was killed by Paris, who wounded him in the heel.

5. Fannie Lou Hamer grew up in the South. Like many other African Americans there, she was poor. Life was hard, and her people had few rights. In 1962 Fannie was fed up. She wanted to change things. She registered to vote but was arrested for no reason. Bullets were fired at her. She was even beaten. Still she worked to gain voting rights for all people. In 1965 her dream came true. Congress passed a voting-rights bill.

_____ 1. From the story you can tell that Peter Salem
   A. had to become a slave again after the war
   B. joined the British Army
   C. fought for himself and the freedom of his country
   D. was a coward

_____ 2. You can conclude that Texas
   A. changed some of its laws when it became a state
   B. never joined the United States
   C. is a republic today
   D. still uses its own money

_____ 3. The story suggests that
   A. all parents babble
   B. deaf babies learn to communicate by imitating
   C. all parents know sign language
   D. deaf babies babble with their toes

_____ 4. You can tell from the story that
   A. Achilles was not killed at Troy
   B. the river's water was very cold
   C. Achilles should have worn socks
   D. Achilles's mother was unable to protect her son

_____ 5. The story suggests that Fannie Lou Hamer
   A. liked being poor
   B. was arrested for running a stop sign
   C. never achieved her goal
   D. had a dangerous fight to win her rights

1. Why do some dogs bark all the time? Some experts believe that dogs communicate through their barking. Other experts believe that dogs bark just to make noise. A new study supports this second view. The study suggests that dogs are wolves that just never grew up. Although dogs and wolves have the same ancestors, modern dogs behave in much the same ways as wolf pups, which bark all the time. On the other hand, older wolves seldom bark.

2. Golda Meir was born in the Soviet Union, and as a girl she moved to the United States. Then as a young woman, Golda moved again, only this time she went to Palestine. There she worked very hard to found the new Jewish nation of Israel. In 1948 her dream finally came true when Israel became a nation. Twenty years later Golda Meir became the leader of Israel.

3. Have you ever watched a caterpillar crawl? Although its crawling seems easy enough, it takes great effort. The caterpillar has more than two thousand muscles, and it must use most of these muscles just to move. A human being has only about seven hundred muscles. So moving is really much easier for a human being.

4. As a boy Alberto Santos-Dumont loved to work with motors. By age 12 he could run the train on his father's coffee farm in Brazil. Six years later he went to France to study flying. In 1898 he made the world's first powered flight. His airship was a giant, cigar-shaped bag filled with hydrogen that was powered by a small gasoline engine.

5. The Navajo people believed that death was necessary to make the sun move. If the sun moved, then someone had to die. But of course, the Navajo did not want to die. Then a wise man told them a tale. He said that in death they simply moved to another world. They would still sit by the river and enjoy themselves.

_____ **1.** From the story you can tell that

    A. all experts agree on why dogs bark

    B. the study claims that dogs bark to communicate

    C. old wolves bark all the time

    D. the study suggests that dogs bark for no real reason

_____ **2.** You can conclude that Golda Meir

    A. became leader of Israel because of her hard work

    B. was born in Palestine

    C. became leader when she was a young girl

    D. became the leader of the Soviet Union

_____ **3.** From the story you can tell that

    A. humans have more muscles than caterpillars

    B. caterpillars have more muscles than humans

    C. humans like to crawl

    D. crawling is very easy for caterpillars

_____ **4.** From the story you can tell that Santos-Dumont

    A. hated motors

    B. was the first man to fly an airship with a motor

    C. went to France when he was 12

    D. used an engine that ran on hydrogen

_____ **5.** The story tells that the Navajo

    A. wanted to die

    B. became the sun when they died

    C. believed that death was not so bad

    D. would suffer when they died

1. In 1991 death caught up with James Bell. But as a young man, "Cool Papa" Bell was the fastest baseball player in the African American leagues. He sometimes played as many as 3 games a day during his 29 seasons as a ball player. Ninety dollars a month is not much of a salary, yet he loved the game. Although his skills were well known, he was never invited to join the big leagues. In 1974 he was voted into the Baseball Hall of Fame.

2. Winds are caused by the uneven heating of the earth's surface. As this uneven heating takes place, differences in air pressure occur. These differences in air pressure cause air to rush from one pressure zone to another. This rush of air is known as wind.

3. Simón Bolívar is known as a champion of freedom in South America. He was born in 1783. At the time most of the continent was ruled by Spain, whose rulers were cruel and unjust. As a young man, Bolívar began to fight for freedom. He died in 1830. But in his life, he helped free six nations. One of these nations was Bolivia, which was named for him.

4. Ray Ragsdale was just a regular high-school student in Texas. He liked sports and was a good athlete. But then he discovered that he had cancer in his right leg. Ragsdale had several treatments to kill the cancer, but these were not successful. The leg had to be removed. But Ragsdale fought back from his loss and returned to the sports he enjoyed. He played both football and baseball. Of course, he couldn't run, but he could hop forty yards in less than nine seconds!

5. High on a hill in the center of Athens, Greece, is a place called the Acropolis. This place is made up of several buildings. This would not be unusual, but most of these buildings are more than two thousand years old. They were built as temples to the ancient Greek gods. The most famous of these buildings is the Parthenon.

_____ **1.** From the story you can tell that James Bell

    A. became rich by playing baseball

    B. was a slow runner

    C. played baseball only for a short while

    D. was honored for his baseball skills

_____ **2.** You can tell from the story that

    A. uneven heating causes snow

    B. winds are caused by the spinning of the earth

    C. uneven heating causes differences in pressure

    D. the earth's surface is on fire

_____ **3.** You can conclude that

    A. Bolívar was honored for his struggle

    B. the Spanish rulers wanted people to be free

    C. Bolívar liked the Spanish rulers

    D. the Spanish rulers liked Bolívar

_____ **4.** The story suggests that Ray Ragsdale

    A. quit playing sports

    B. just wanted to have a regular life

    C. could run fast

    D. played tennis and soccer

_____ **5.** You can conclude that the Acropolis

    A. was an important place in ancient Athens

    B. was once a football stadium

    C. no longer has buildings in it

    D. was built as a hamburger stand

1. When people marry they often exchange wedding rings. The rings are symbols of the love that the married couple share. But in many marriages, only the woman wears a ring. This practice goes back to ancient times. During that time many wives were captured or bought. These women wore rings to show that they were the property of their husbands.

2. Chiang Kai-shek was a famous Chinese leader. As a young man, he gained much power in China. He led the Chinese Army against the Japanese in World War II. After the war the Communists tried to take over China. Kai-shek fought bravely against them, but he lost the fight. With his followers he fled to Taiwan. Until his death he continued to fight against the Communist rule of China.

3. Seashores experience a daily change in water level. This change is called tide. As the water is pulled from shore, the water level drops. This is known as low tide. As the water returns to shore, the water level rises. This is called high tide. The coming and going of the water is caused by the pull of the moon's gravity.

4. Have you ever looked up a word in a dictionary? Well, you can thank Noah Webster. He worked almost all his life to make American spelling fit a standard. He produced two large books of words. The larger one appeared in 1828. Webster's work has been improved many times. His dictionary is still in use today.

5. Carbon dioxide in the atmosphere acts as a blanket. It lets light pass through, but it traps heat. This occurrence is called the greenhouse effect. It is rather good, for without it the earth would be much colder. But as the carbon dioxide increases, the heat of the earth's surface rises. This isn't good. Carbon dioxide comes from the burning of oil, coal, and gasoline. If we do not limit this burning, the world may suffer as a result.

_____ **1.** You can conclude that

    A. most wives are still purchased today

    B. the meaning of some wedding customs
has changed

    C. wedding rings are worn in the nose

    D. couples should no longer marry

_____ **2.** The story suggests that Chiang Kai-shek

    A. believed that China should remain a free country

    B. is still the leader of China

    C. fled to Japan

    D. was a Communist

_____ **3.** You can tell from the story that

    A. tides are caused by the gravity of the sun

    B. the water level drops at high tide

    C. the moon has a strong effect on the earth's seas

    D. a *tide* is a change in water temperature

_____ **4.** You can conclude that Noah Webster

    A. respected and loved the American language

    B. didn't know how to spell

    C. liked to write long letters

    D. couldn't read

_____ **5.** From this story you can tell that

    A. carbon dioxide traps light

    B. the earth would be warmer without the
greenhouse effect

    C. the greenhouse effect is never good

    D. too much carbon dioxide is bad

1. Many cities hold distance races called marathons. Runners gather from around the country. They race through the streets, up and down hills, and over bridges. People who want something different can go run a marathon in Indiana. The runners there dash down the dark passages of the Merengo Cave!

2. Moths are related to butterflies. However, most moths fly at night. Butterflies fly during the day. When a moth is resting, it folds its wings back over its body. A butterfly, on the other hand, holds its wings upward.

3. White eggs and brown eggs taste exactly the same. In some places, however, people think that brown eggs are better. They are willing to pay more money for them. For example, in Boston brown eggs usually cost more than they do in New York.

4. Inventors record their inventions with the government. The inventors hope that someone will buy their bright ideas. But some inventions are so strange that no one wants them. Government files show inventions for odd things, such as flying fire escapes and eyeglasses for chickens. There is even an alarm clock that hits the sleeping person on the head with a piece of wood!

5. The sidewinder is a kind of snake that lives in the desert. Unlike other snakes the sidewinder does not crawl. Instead, it coils its body into big loops. Then suddenly it unwinds itself. The snake skims over the sand much like a leaf in the wind. It moves forward and slightly sideways at the same time.

_____ **1.** From this story you can tell that

    A. all marathons are alike

    B. most runners like cave races

    C. Merengo Cave must be pretty long

    D. marathons are bicycle races

_____ **2.** This story tells

    A. how moths and butterflies are alike

    B. how moths and butterflies are different

    C. why people confuse moths and butterflies

    D. why moths are better than butterflies

_____ **3.** You could conclude that people in New York

    A. don't eat brown eggs

    B. think brown eggs are best

    C. eat more eggs than people eat in Boston

    D. think white eggs are better

_____ **4.** The story tells about inventions that

    A. do not work

    B. were turned down by the government

    C. have been used in many places

    D. did not make any money

_____ **5.** The sidewinder gets its name from

    A. the place in which it lives

    B. the direction in which it moves

    C. the fact that it moves easily

    D. a group of other snakes

1. Many children are familiar with Mother Goose rhymes. Historians aren't sure whether or not Mother Goose was a real person. Some say that her real name was Elizabeth Vergoose. They believe Vergoose is buried in Boston, Massachusetts. Historians think that her son published a book of her songs and rhymes. But such a book has never been found.

2. In our alphabet, *G* is the seventh letter. It was the third letter in the alphabet of the ancient Greeks. In addition to its main use in forming words, *G* is sometimes used to stand for other words and things. If you are measuring weight, small *g* stands for *gram*. In music, *G* is the name of the note that follows *F*.

3. Columns and columns of rock stand along the coast of Ireland. They make up a natural wonder called the Giant's Causeway. An old story says that this bridge was built by a character named Finn MacCool. He was building a bridge so that giants could walk from Ireland to Scotland.

4. Our Constitution gives people freedom of speech. But that does not mean that people can say whatever they want. What if someone was in a store and wanted to cause trouble? The person could shout "Fire!" even if there wasn't any fire. Everyone would run out of the store at once, and people could get hurt. In this case the guilty person would not be protected under the freedom-of-speech laws.

5. The porcupine uses the quills on its tail to defend itself. When an animal comes too close, the porcupine slaps its tail at the enemy. The sharp quills come off easily. They stick into the other creature's skin. Each quill has a hook at the end. This makes the quills very painful to remove.

_____ **1.** From this story you can tell that

    A. Elizabeth Vergoose wrote a book

    B. the truth about Mother Goose remains a mystery

    C. there was never a real person called Mother Goose

    D. no one tells Mother Goose tales anymore

_____ **2.** From this story you <u>cannot</u> tell

    A. how to pronounce *G* in English

    B. which things *G* stands for

    C. which place *G* has in the alphabet

    D. what *G* is mainly used for

_____ **3.** From this story you can tell that

    A. the causeway must be small

    B. the causeway must be new

    C. MacCool didn't really build the causeway

    D. giants still walk across the causeway

_____ **4.** You can conclude that our laws

    A. are unfair to people

    B. cause trouble in stores

    C. may not protect people who lie

    D. let people say whatever they want

_____ **5.** If the quills didn't have hooks, they would

    A. not stay on the porcupine

    B. come out more easily

    C. hurt much more

    D. shoot through the air

1. The first eyeglasses were probably made in China. With the printing of books in Europe in the 1400s, more people needed glasses. Ben Franklin invented bifocal glasses. The lenses on these glasses have two parts. One section is designed to correct for close vision, while the other section corrects for distant vision.

2. The king of gnomes is Gob, who rules with a magic sword. Gnomes are peculiar-looking, little creatures who live underground and wear long beards. It is said that gnomes guard large treasures. It is also said that gnomes have the power to make people feel sad.

3. You've probably bought a soft drink from a vending machine. Did you ever wonder how the machine knows that you're using a real coin, such as a dime? When you put your dime in the slot, the machine weighs the coin. If its weight is correct, the machine then measures its size. Finally the machine makes sure that there are notches on the edge of the dime.

4. Have you ever seen barnacles on a dock or a boat? When these shellfish are small, they have only 1 eye and 6 pairs of legs. As they get older, they have 2 more eyes, 12 pairs of legs, and 2 big feelers. In their final stage of growth, barnacles lose their eyes and attach themselves to another object for the rest of their lives.

5. Years ago, people kept bread even if there was mold growing on it. Although they didn't eat this bread, they placed the spoiled bread on wounds. The mold helped the wounds heal. Today we call this mold penicillin. It is used to kill many kinds of germs. Penicillin is now made in laboratories and saves millions of lives each year.

_____ **1.** You can conclude that before the 1400s

    A. most people wore glasses

    B. most people had good eyesight

    C. people didn't read much

    D. many people wore bifocals

_____ **2.** From this story you can tell that gnomes

    A. are make-believe

    B. have made very much money

    C. are helpful to people

    D. carry swords

_____ **3.** You can conclude that vending machines

    A. aren't easy to fool

    B. don't take real dimes

    C. accept coins smaller than dimes

    D. accept wooden dimes

_____ **4.** From this story you can tell that barnacles

    A. remain the same throughout their lives

    B. can see better when they are old

    C. pass through three stages of life

    D. are delicious to eat

_____ **5.** From the story you <u>cannot</u> tell

    A. how moldy bread was used in the past

    B. what penicillin can do

    C. how penicillin got its name

    D. where scientists make penicillin

1. Some people love a good story. Once every year a group of people get together for a story-telling festival. They take turns entertaining each other by spinning yarns and swapping tales.

2. In the making of a baseball, machines do most of the work. One machine covers a piece of cork with rubber. Another machine wraps yarn around the ball. The leather used to cover the ball is also cut by a machine. But people are still needed to sew the leather covers on the balls by hand.

3. Many animals shed their outer coverings every year. Then they grow new ones. Birds lose their feathers and grow new, colorful ones. Snakes lose their old skins. New, shiny skin forms underneath the old skin. Some mammals lose part of their hair in warm weather. But they grow heavy coats in cold weather.

4. By noting changes, a lie-detector machine shows whether someone is lying. The machine shows changes in heartbeat and breathing. These changes might take place when a person is lying. But these changes also take place when a person is nervous. Sometimes a person is lying but doesn't know it. In this case the machine doesn't note any change at all.

5. Our country once had a state named for Benjamin Franklin. It was at the time that North Carolina gave some land to the new government. But the land was later returned to North Carolina. Today that land is part of the state of Tennessee.

1. You can tell that

    A. storytellers like wool

    B. the festival has many activities

    C. the festival is dull

    D. storytellers like to share stories

2. You can tell that machines

    A. probably can't sew leather covers on balls

    B. always get tangled up in the yarn

    C. make the cork used for making balls

    D. can't cover cork with rubber

3. Some mammals lose part of their hair

    A. so that they can grow larger

    B. in order to keep cool

    C. when cold weather is on the way

    D. when they are babies

4. From the story you <u>cannot</u> tell

    A. what happens when a person lies

    B. what a lie detector shows

    C. which changes take place when a person is nervous

    D. how a lie detector is used in court

5. From the story you <u>cannot</u> tell

    A. who Benjamin Franklin was

    B. where the state was located

    C. when we had a state named for Franklin

    D. what happened to the state

1. Do you have trouble remembering the words to our national song? If you were a citizen of Greece, you might have even more trouble. The Greek national song has 158 verses. Most Greeks know only the first 4 verses. But if you lived in Kuwait, you wouldn't have any problem at all. Kuwait's song hasn't any words.

2. There's a giant buffalo sculpture in Jamestown, North Dakota. It's made of steel and concrete, and it weighs sixty tons. In Houston, Texas, there's a large shrimp. It's twenty feet tall. The world's largest bull is found in Audubon, Iowa. The statue stands in farm country.

3. Many radio stations have contests. People call the station to answer the questions they hear on the air. The prize might be money, a T-shirt, or even tickets to a show. One New York station had the same winner one hundred times!

4. Long ago, people in Egypt picked wild olives. They rubbed the oil of this fruit on their skins. They also burned the oil in their lamps. The workers who built the pyramids put olive oil under the huge stones. This made the stones easier to move. Hundreds of years later, people in Syria began to grow olives for food.

5. In 1892 people working for a magazine wanted to celebrate Columbus Day. Francis Bellamy wrote a statement titled the "Pledge of Allegiance to the Flag" for the magazine. Through the years this pledge became very popular. It is still recited today.

_____ **1.** You can tell from the story that

- **A.** Americans are not good at learning songs
- **B.** people in Kuwait do not like to sing
- **C.** Greeks do not like their national song
- **D.** national songs are different in every country

_____ **2.** From the story you can conclude that

- **A.** buffalo still roam in Texas
- **B.** the sculptures are found in museums
- **C.** the same sculptor made all the statues
- **D.** Americans must like huge statues of animals

_____ **3.** From the story you <u>cannot</u> tell

- **A.** what the prizes are
- **B.** what the contest questions are like
- **C.** where the people hear the questions
- **D.** the number of times that one person won

_____ **4.** The people of ancient Egypt probably didn't

- **A.** eat olives
- **B.** build many buildings
- **C.** think olives were valuable
- **D.** know how to grow crops

_____ **5.** Before 1892 Americans didn't

- **A.** celebrate Columbus Day
- **B.** read magazines
- **C.** honor the flag
- **D.** say the "Pledge of Allegiance"

1. When Bessie Smith was a young girl, both of her parents died. But Smith's love of music helped her through hard times. By the age of nine, Smith was singing on street corners for spare change, and ten years later, Smith was singing the blues in cities throughout the South. Despite a life full of trouble and hardship, Smith managed to survive because of her music. Before her death in 1937, she was known throughout the world as the Empress of the Blues.

2. Born in Costa Rica, Franklin Chang-Díaz dreamed all his young life of flying in space. At the age of 17, he moved to the United States. He couldn't speak English, but he learned it quickly and became a top student. Then in 1980 Franklin was selected as an astronaut. He trained hard to reach his goal. In 1986 his boyhood dream came true. He soared through space on the shuttle *Columbia*.

3. The parachute is not a modern invention. Two hundred years ago, Andre Garnerin of France used one for the first time. A balloon lifted him high into the sky. Then he cut the cord that held him to the balloon. For a while he fell very rapidly, but then he suddenly slowed down because the parachute began unfolding. As a crowd looked on in awe, he landed safely on the ground.

4. Black holes are regions of space from which nothing can escape. The gravity of black holes is so strong that even light can't escape. Black holes are caused mostly by stars that cave in upon themselves and whose mass is decreased to a very small size. As their size shrinks, their gravity grows stronger.

5. Scientists know that cars and factories cause pollution. This pollution can make the earth's heat rise. But did you know that the belching of cows is also a problem? When cows belch, they produce the gas methane. Methane can worsen the greenhouse effect.

_____ **1.** From the story you can tell that Smith

  A. was rewarded for her love of music
  B. couldn't sing very well
  C. had a happy childhood
  D. is still alive today

_____ **2.** From this story you <u>cannot</u> tell

  A. where Chang-Díaz was born
  B. about the boyhood dream of Chang-Díaz
  C. how many astronauts flew with Chang-Díaz
  D. when Chang-Díaz flew in space

_____ **3.** You can conclude that

  A. Garnerin fell to his death
  B. the crowd had seen many parachutes before
  C. Garnerin's parachute didn't open
  D. the crowd was amazed by Garnerin's landing

_____ **4.** The story suggests that black holes

  A. are dug by Martians
  B. are black because light can't escape from them
  C. occur on the ocean floor
  D. are caused by comets

_____ **5.** From the story you <u>cannot</u> tell

  A. which things cause pollution
  B. what cow belching produces
  C. whether cow belching is a problem
  D. how many times a cow belches each day

1.   Do you like vanilla ice cream? This tasty treat gets its flavor from the vanilla bean. Many vanilla beans come from vines in Mexico. The beans are slender, yellow pods full of tiny, black seeds. In fact, *vanilla* means "little pod" in Spanish. The beans are picked and cured by heating. Then they are chopped and mixed with alcohol. The vanilla flavoring is then strained and bottled.

2.   Mary Cassatt was a famous American painter. She was born in 1844. As a girl she traveled to Paris. There she gained a love of painting. As a young woman, she returned to Paris to study art. Her talent soon became well known. She painted mostly women and children in daily life. Around 1900 her eyesight began to fail. Her artwork suffered greatly. By World War I, her eyesight was so poor that she could no longer paint at all.

3.   Most places on the seashore have two daily tides. They are known as high tide and low tide. Usually the difference between the water level of these two tides is only three or four feet. But a place in Canada has a great difference in tides. At the Bay of Fundy in Nova Scotia, the difference in tides is more than fifty feet.

4.   As a young man, Jesse Treviño was a skilled artist. He won several art contests. But in 1966 Treviño had to join the army. He was sent to fight in Vietnam. There he was wounded badly. His drawing hand had to be removed. But Treviño struggled to overcome this loss. Finally he learned to draw with a mechanical arm. Treviño is a successful artist today.

5.   The people of the world speak many different languages. This can cause problems. There are some people who have tried to make up one language for the whole world. The best try at a world language was that of a Russian doctor. He called it Esperanto. But it never gained widespread use.

_____ **1.** From the story you <u>cannot</u> tell

    A. where vanilla beans come from

    B. how much flavoring is put in vanilla ice cream

    C. what *vanilla* means in Spanish

    D. how vanilla beans are cured

_____ **2.** You can conclude that

    A. Mary's talent suffered because of her blindness

    B. Mary joined the army in World War I

    C. most of Mary's paintings were of soldiers

    D. Mary's paintings were not very good

_____ **3.** The story suggests that the Bay of Fundy

    A. is in South Carolina

    B. has ten tides daily

    C. is not near the seashore

    D. has unusual tides

_____ **4.** You can tell from the story that Treviño

    A. gave up art

    B. did not go to Vietnam

    C. was wounded in his hand

    D. never recovered from his wound

_____ **5.** From the story you <u>cannot</u> tell

    A. what Esperanto is

    B. who developed Esperanto

    C. whether Esperanto was ever widely used

    D. how many different languages people speak today

1. As a child Richard Wright had a hard life. As an adult he decided to become a writer, since he had always loved to read. Because he was African American, he wasn't sure that he could achieve his dream. He worked many jobs while he wrote stories about hatred and racial problems. His first book of stories appeared in 1937. It was a great success. Wright became a major writer in spite of his doubts.

2. Many people like to keep bees as a hobby. Others sell the honey that bees make. But beekeeping has its strange beliefs. According to one belief, bees feel that they are important members of the beekeeper's household. If they are not told of family events, they leave the hive. Also, if not treated right, the luck of the family vanishes along with the bees.

3. Have you ever been blamed for making a mess? The word *mess* comes from Latin and means "to send." At first, *mess* meant "a portion of food sent or served." Later it came to mean "a dish sent for several people." In some cases *mess* still means "dish." An example is the mess kit used by soldiers in the army.

4. Mild winds do not blow very hard. These winds are good for sailing or flying a kite. They also help keep you cool on hot days. But strong winds can be very dangerous. The strongest surface wind ever measured was in New Hampshire. The wind roared there at 231 miles per hour in 1934!

5. Plants are born, grow, create young, and die just as animals do. Plants known as annuals complete this cycle in just one year. They produce many seeds at one time. Plants known as perennials take years to reach full growth. This second type produces only a few seeds at a time.

1. From the story you <u>cannot</u> tell
  A. what kind of childhood Wright had
  B. whether Wright became a successful writer
  C. when Wright's first book appeared
  D. the title of Wright's first book

2. From this story you can tell that
  A. some people treat bees like people
  B. bees do not produce honey
  C. a beekeeper should treat bees badly
  D. bees always mean bad luck

3. The story suggests that *mess*
  A. now means "soldier"
  B. is a Greek word
  C. has many meanings
  D. once meant "a light rain"

4. From the story you <u>cannot</u> tell
  A. where the strongest wind blew
  B. how fast the wind blew in New Hampshire
  C. if anyone flew a kite in the strongest wind
  D. when the strongest wind blew

5. You can tell from the story that
  A. annuals live many years
  B. perennials live longer than annuals
  C. annuals are animals
  D. perennials produce many seeds at a time

1. The belief in lucky horseshoes dates back thousands of years. The Semites had a goddess named Astarte. She was the goddess of love and beauty, and the horseshoe was her symbol. The Semites believed that there was a special way of handling the horseshoe. The shoe had to be hung with its points upward for good luck.

2. William Bligh was the cruel captain of a ship named the *Bounty*. He treated his sailors very badly. In 1789 the sailors couldn't take any more cruelty. By staging a mutiny and taking control of the ship, they put Bligh and 18 others into a small boat. But Bligh was able to sail the boat 4,000 miles across the Pacific to safety.

3. There was a small Russian girl at the 1972 Olympics. She stood bravely before a huge audience and began her performance. She tumbled, leaped, flipped, and danced. She did somersaults and other difficult gymnastics exercises. In spite of her clean moves, the small girl did not win any medals at the end of the contest. But Olga Korbut had won the hearts of people all over the world.

4. When forests are buried under mud and ash from volcanoes, the wood in the trees changes form. After a while the wood becomes as hard as rock. It is then known as petrified wood. There are several petrified forests in the United States. The most famous one is in the Painted Desert near the Grand Canyon.

5. The Trail of Tears marked a sad event in Native American history. The Cherokee tribe lived in the southeast part of the country. But white settlers wanted them to move. The government ordered the Cherokee to leave their homes. They were told to move to Oklahoma. They didn't want to leave, but after some time they agreed. The trip was long and hard. Finally in March 1839, the tribe reached its new home. But more than three thousand Cherokee had died on the trip.

_____ **1.** From this story you <u>cannot</u> tell

    A. how to hang a horseshoe for good luck

    B. about the goddess whose symbol was the horseshoe

    C. if a lucky horseshoe needed to be new or used

    D. about the name of the Semite goddess

_____ **2.** The story suggests that Captain Bligh

    A. was a good sailor

    B. treated his crew well

    C. was popular with his crew

    D. did not lose control of his ship

_____ **3.** You can conclude that

    A. Korbut was a weightlifter

    B. the crowd cheered for Korbut

    C. Korbut won a gold medal

    D. the small girl fell down often

_____ **4.** From the story you <u>cannot</u> tell

    A. how wood becomes petrified

    B. what petrified wood is like

    C. if volcanoes help form petrified wood

    D. the state in which the Painted Desert is found

_____ **5.** You can tell from the story that

    A. the Cherokee liked their home in the southeast

    B. the tribe enjoyed the long journey

    C. the Cherokee never reached Oklahoma

    D. the white settlers liked the Cherokee

1. The man carefully eyed the painting in the flea market. The picture was torn, but the frame was in good shape. The man decided to pay the asking price of four dollars. Later when the man removed the picture from the frame, he found an old piece of paper. The man's eyes widened in surprise because he had found an original copy of the Declaration of Independence. It was worth one million dollars!

2. Mary Bacon loved to ride horses, and she turned that love into a job. Being one of the first female jockeys, Mary rode her horses to many wins, but she also experienced many setbacks. One time she was thrown from a horse and broke her back. Another time a horse fell on top of her. But each time she returned to race again. She once said, "You can't quit just because you've been thrown."

3. Charles Edensaw was a member of the Haida tribe. He lived in western Canada. Edensaw became a fine artist. He used wood, gold, and silver in his works. He was also a talented crafter of argillite, which is a kind of shale. His art included drawings, sketches, pipes, and totem poles. Today many of his works are found in museums.

4. Sonja Henie was one of the best ice-skaters of all time. Her first major contest was the 1924 Winter Olympics. Henie was just 12 years old! She won gold medals in the next 3 Olympics. She even won 10 world titles in a row. Then Henie became a movie star. Her movies often showed her skating. As a result, ice-skating was soon a popular sport around the world.

5. In Zuni legends the home was the center of *itiwana*, which meant "the world." The Zuni believed that everything in the world was alive. Everything was one and had to be kept in balance. That could be done only through prayer and with the help of the gods. So the Zuni held many ceremonies and asked for help from the gods.

_____ **1.** You can conclude that

    A. the man always had rotten luck

    B. the old piece of paper was a restaurant menu

    C. the man was glad that he bought the painting

    D. the frame was worth one million dollars

_____ **2.** From the story you <u>cannot</u> tell

    A. about Mary's job

    B. which horse threw Mary in 1969

    C. if Mary returned to racing after her accidents

    D. how Mary broke her back

_____ **3.** From this story you can tell that

    A. Charles Edensaw was a successful artist

    B. all of Edensaw's works are missing today

    C. Edensaw used only crayons in his works

    D. the Haida tribe lived in Kansas

_____ **4.** From the story you <u>cannot</u> tell

    A. which sport Henie was best at

    B. how many movies Henie made

    C. when Henie's first major contest took place

    D. how many world titles Henie won in a row

_____ **5.** The story suggests that the Zuni

    A. lived in motels

    B. thought prayer would make their homes fall down

    C. believed everything in the world was dead

    D. thought they needed the gods' help for a good life

1. Aaron Burr is remembered as one man who almost became President of the United States. He had been successful in life. He had been a soldier and a lawyer. He became a senator at age 35. Then he ran for President against Thomas Jefferson. The number of votes for the 2 men was equal. So the House of Representatives had to make the decision as to who would become leader. Burr lost.

2. Wind and water often work to wear down rock. This process of nature is called erosion. There is a machine called a rock tumbler that can do the same thing. Rocks are placed inside a small barrel. A motor turns the barrel, and the rocks grind against each other. It takes nature thousands of years to make a rock smooth. But a rock tumbler can achieve the same result in a month.

3. Wyomia Tyus loved to run. This love won her many honors. She was African American and born in Georgia in 1945. She ran track in high school and college. She went on to win gold and silver medals in the 1964 Olympics. Tyus returned to the Olympics four years later. There she showed her great talent once again. She won two more gold medals for her efforts.

4. The early Navajo lived in an earth-covered dwelling called a hogan. The hogan was circle-shaped. Its framework was made of forked poles. The poles were covered with branches, brush, and soil. The hogan was always built to face east. The Navajo believed that the Holy People had built the first hogan in this way.

5. Some people think that Friday is an unlucky day. But many key things in American history have taken place on this day. Columbus set sail for the New World on a Friday. It was on a Friday that he found the mainland of North America. The Pilgrims reached the new land on a Friday. Also, George Washington was born on a Friday.

_____ **1.** The story suggests that Aaron Burr

    A. was a total failure

    B. liked to get haircuts

    C. was never President of the United States

    D. received more votes than Jefferson

_____ **2.** From this story you can tell that

    A. rock tumblers imitate the process of erosion

    B. nature works faster than a rock tumbler

    C. rock tumblers make rocks jagged

    D. wind and water make rocks bigger

_____ **3.** From the story you <u>cannot</u> tell

    A. where Tyus was born

    B. in which Olympics Tyus took part

    C. how many gold medals Tyus won

    D. what kind of track races Tyus won

_____ **4.** You can conclude that the Navajo

    A. also built skyscrapers

    B. used bricks to build their hogans

    C. tried to be like the Holy People

    D. ate with forked poles

_____ **5.** From the story you <u>cannot</u> tell

    A. on which day Washington was born

    B. why people think Friday is an unlucky day

    C. which continent was discovered by Columbus

    D. on which day the Pilgrims reached America

1. Sandra Day O'Connor attended college and became a lawyer. But after she graduated, she couldn't find a job. Most law firms wouldn't hire female lawyers. O'Connor wanted to change this unfairness. First she was elected to the Arizona Senate. Then she became a judge. She was chosen to serve on the United States Supreme Court in 1981 and became the first woman to achieve this honor.

2. Have you ever had a nightmare? This kind of horrible dream can cause you to wake up screaming and breathing hard. The word *nightmare* comes from an ancient Saxon legend. The Saxons believed that Mara was an evil spirit that crouched on the chests of sleeping people and made their sleep very uncomfortable.

3. Hazel Wightman was one of America's early tennis champions. She first played the game in 1902. Six months later she won her first tournament. Her last tournament win took place more than 50 years later. During her years of play, she came up with many new ways to play the game better. She used her skills to teach others how to play. Wightman was still teaching tennis when she died at age 87.

4. Chief Joseph was a leader of the Nez Perce tribe. His tribe lived in a valley in Oregon. White settlers began moving into their land. The Nez Perce were ordered to move, but they refused. They decided to fight and then run away. They hoped to reach freedom in Canada. But they didn't make it. In 1877 Chief Joseph was forced to surrender. Tearfully he said, "My heart is sick and sad. From where the sun now stands, I will fight no more forever."

5. In 1421 war swept across the small country of Bohemia. Troops met on the battlefield many times. One of the best generals in the war was John Zizka. He led his troops to 12 major victories. The amazing thing was that Zizka was totally blind!

_____ **1.** From the story you <u>cannot</u> tell

    A. what Sandra O'Connor studied in college

    B. for which state she was senator

    C. when she joined the Supreme Court

    D. which college O'Connor attended

_____ **2.** You can tell from the story that

    A. nightmares were named after Mara

    B. Mara was a spirit in Spanish legends

    C. nightmares make people happy

    D. Mara sat on the pillows of sleeping people

_____ **3.** The story suggests that

    A. Wightman is still alive

    B. tennis played a big part in Wightman's life

    C. Wightman was never very good at tennis

    D. Wightman played tennis only for a short while

_____ **4.** From the story you <u>cannot</u> tell

    A. which tribe Chief Joseph led

    B. where Chief Joseph's tribe lived

    C. what happened to Chief Joseph after he surrendered

    D. whether Chief Joseph's tribe ever reached Canada

_____ **5.** You can conclude that John Zizka

    A. lived in Bohemia

    B. had perfect vision

    C. never won any battles

    D. was hated by his troops

1. The Ghost Dance is a traditional dance among many Native American tribes. Legend claims that the dance was begun by a Paiute named Wovoka, who had spoken to the Great Spirit. The Great Spirit advised the Paiute to be good and to live in peace. He presented Wovoka with the dance and told him that if the tribe danced for five nights, they would gain happiness. He also told him that the spirits of the dead would join the tribe.

2. For many years bowling alleys were not considered proper places for women, but Floretta McCutcheon changed all that. She began bowling in 1923, and within four years she was the best bowler in her town. Then she challenged Jimmy Smith, the world champion. When the match was over, Floretta had won! Later she toured the nation, giving lessons and putting on bowling shows. She had many bowling fans.

3. In the 1860s two crews set out to build a railroad. It would cross the western United States. One crew started laying tracks in Nebraska. The other crew began its work in California. Building the railroad took four years. The two crews met at Promontory Point, Utah, in May 1869. A golden spike was driven into the ground. The spike honored the completion of the railroad.

4. As a young man, John Baird felt that he was a failure. He had never held a job very long. He had been an engineer and a sales clerk. He was still poor and discouraged. But he liked conducting experiments in his attic lab. His goal was to send pictures by way of electricity. In 1926 he was successful. His efforts gave us television.

5. Leo Fender became a legend before his death in 1991. He made electric guitars. One kind is still played by great rock guitarists today. It is called the Fender Stratocaster. Guitar players love the way it feels and its sound. But Fender was a strange man. He didn't like rock music much. Nor did he ever learn to play a guitar!

_____ **1.** The story suggests that the Ghost Dance

    A. would bring good luck to a tribe

    B. was danced only by ghosts

    C. was given to Wovoka by the Great Turtle

    D. would cause people to die

_____ **2.** From the story you <u>cannot</u> tell

    A. when McCutcheon began to bowl

    B. which world champion McCutcheon defeated

    C. the town in which McCutcheon lived

    D. the kind of shows McCutcheon put on

_____ **3.** From the story you can tell that

    A. the railroad crossed western Canada

    B. the two crews worked in directions toward each other

    C. the golden spike was driven in Nebraska

    D. Promontory Point is in California

_____ **4.** From the story you <u>cannot</u> tell

    A. which kinds of jobs John Baird held

    B. why John Baird was discouraged

    C. when John Baird first broadcast pictures

    D. what kind of pictures John Baird first sent

_____ **5.** You can conclude that

    A. making and playing guitars require different skills

    B. Fender is still alive

    C. Fender's guitars were not very good

    D. Fender liked banjo music

Think and Apply

Funny Conclusions

Read the jokes below. Tell how the jokes are funny by answering the questions in the spaces. Use the clues in each joke to support your conclusion.

1. The school principal received a telephone call. The voice said, "Bob Johnson won't be in school today." "Who is this?" asked the principal. "This is my father speaking."

What is the mistake in the phone call?

_____

_____

_____

2. My father was talking to our neighbor. "I'm worried about my daughter's health." "Why? What's wrong with her?" asked the neighbor. "A motorcycle," answered my father.

What does the father think of motorcycles?

_____

_____

_____

3. A man and his friend were in a restaurant. "This is a good restaurant," the man said. "If you order eggs, you get the freshest eggs in the world. If you order hot tea, you get the hottest tea in the world. And . . ." "I believe you," said his friend. "I ordered a small steak."

What is the friend really saying about the steak?

_____

_____

_____

How Are They Alike?

An *analogy* compares things. It shows a connection between two sets of things. The connection is the clue to your conclusion. Look at the example.

A *toe* is to a *foot* as a *finger* is to a *hand*.

In other words, a toe is part of a foot just as a finger is part of a hand.

Read each item below. Ask yourself if there is a connection between the two sets of things. Write *yes* or *no* in the box to tell whether you think the analogy makes sense. Then explain your conclusion on the lines provided.

1. *Window* is to *house* as *porthole* is to *ship*.

_____

_____

2. *Lace* is to *shoe* as *button* is to *table*.

_____

_____

3. *Trunk* is to *elephant* as *snout* is to *pig*.

_____

_____

4. *Cereal* is to *food* as *baseball* is to *sports*.

_____

_____

5. *Feather* is to *bird* as *fur* is to *car*.

_____

_____

To check your answers, turn to page 62.

What About Trout?

Clues help you draw conclusions. The word *trout* appears in each of the lists below. Figure out what a trout has in common with the other items, or clues, in each list. Then draw a conclusion as to why you think *trout* belongs in each list. Write your conclusion on the lines next to each list.

List 1

trout _____

duck _____

diver _____

alligator _____

List 2

trout _____

dog _____

horse _____

elephant _____

List 3

trout _____

tuna _____

shark _____

eel _____

To check your answers, turn to page 62.

✓ Check Yourself

Unit *1* pp. 6-7	Unit *2* pp. 8-9	Unit *3* pp. 10-11	Unit *4* pp. 12-13	Unit *5* pp. 14-15	Unit *6* pp. 16-17	Unit *7* pp. 18-19	Unit *8* pp. 20-21
1. C	1. C	1. D	1. C	1. B	1. A	1. D	1. B
2. A	2. B	2. B	2. C	2. C	2. C	2. A	2. D
3. A	3. A	3. C	3. B	3. D	3. B	3. B	3. A
4. D	4. B	4. A	4. A	4. A	4. A	4. C	4. C
5. D	5. D	5. A	5. D	5. D	5. D	5. A	5. A

Unit 9 pp. 22-23	Unit 10 pp. 24-25	Unit 11 pp. 26-27	Unit 12 pp. 28-29	Unit 13 pp. 30-31	Unit 14 pp. 32-33	Unit 15 pp. 34-35	Unit 16 pp. 36-37
1. C	1. D	1. D	1. B	1. C	1. B	1. C	1. D
2. A	2. A	2. C	2. A	2. B	2. A	2. A	2. A
3. B	3. B	3. A	3. C	3. D	3. C	3. A	3. B
4. D	4. B	4. B	4. A	4. D	4. C	4. C	4. D
5. D	5. C	5. A	5. D	5. B	5. B	5. C	5. A

Unit **17** pp. 38-39	*Unit* **18** pp. 40-41	*Unit* **19** pp. 42-43	*Unit* **20** pp. 44-45	*Unit* **21** pp. 46-47	*Unit* **22** pp. 48-49	*Unit* **23** pp. 50-51	*Unit* **24** pp. 52-53	*Unit* **25** pp. 54-55
1. D	**1.** A	**1.** B	**1.** D	**1.** C	**1.** C	**1.** C	**1.** D	**1.** A
2. D	**2.** C	**2.** A	**2.** A	**2.** A	**2.** B	**2.** A	**2.** A	**2.** C
3. B	**3.** D	**3.** D	**3.** C	**3.** B	**3.** A	**3.** D	**3.** B	**3.** B
4. A	**4.** B	**4.** C	**4.** C	**4.** D	**4.** B	**4.** C	**4.** C	**4.** D
5. D	**5.** D	**5.** D	**5.** B	**5.** A	**5.** D	**5.** B	**5.** A	**5.** A

Using What You Know, Page 3
geography, mathematics, English, art

Practice Drawing Conclusions, Page 4
2. B

Funny Conclusions, Page 56
1. Bob's father wouldn't say, "This is my father speaking."

2. He thinks they are unsafe.

3. The friend is saying that the steak was very small.

How Are They Alike? Page 57
1. Yes. They are both things from which you can look out.

2. No. A lace keeps a shoe tied together. A button cannot hold a table together.

3. Yes. Both are kinds of noses found on animals.

4. Yes. Cereal is a kind of food, and baseball is a kind of sport.

5. No. A feather is a covering for a bird, but fur is not a covering for a car.

What About Trout? Page 58
List 1: They all swim in water.

List 2: They are all animals.

List 3: They are all fish.